T0131926

$5,050 AT 6

KAY JAY

Copyright © 2023 by Kay Jay. 855644

All rights reserved. No part of this book may
be reproduced or transmitted in any form or by
any means, electronic or mechanical, including
photocopying, recording, or by any information storage
and retrieval system, without permission in writing from
the copyright owner.

To order additional copies of this book, contact:
Xlibris
844-714-8691
www.Xlibris.com
Orders@Xlibris.com

ISBN: Softcover   979-8-3694-0763-9
         Hardcover   979-8-3694-0764-6
         EBook   979-8-3694-0762-2

Library of Congress Control Number: 2023917580

Print information available on the last page

Rev. date: 09/15/2023

My name is Nova. I am six years old. One Sunday, I was not feeling well. Aunt Trina was talking to me. I was looking uninterested.

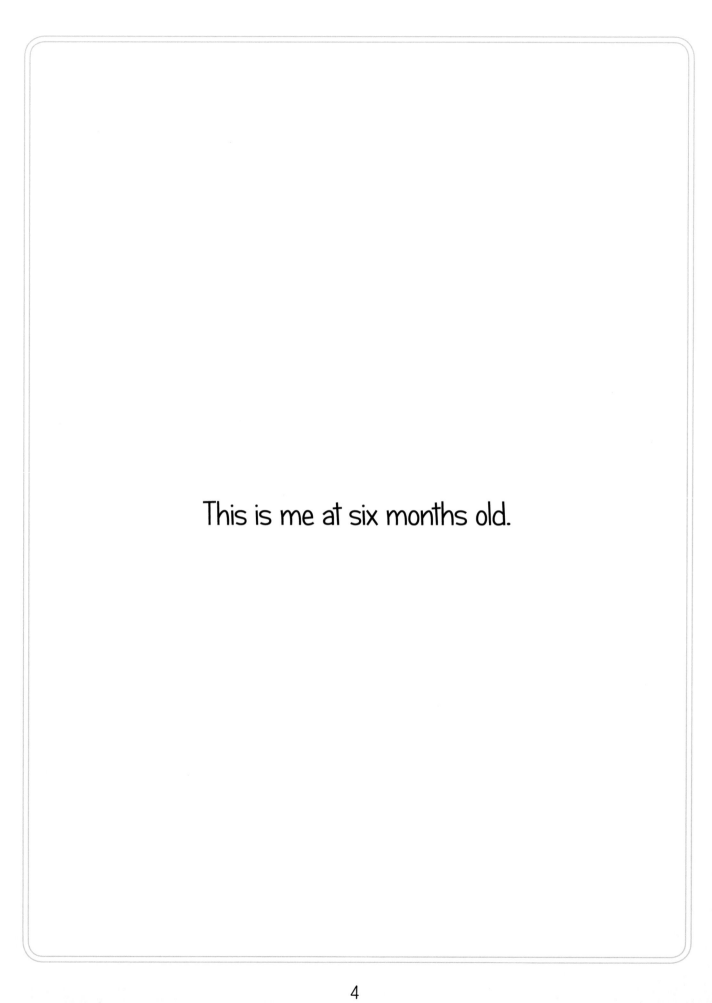

This is me at six months old.

Hey, hey, hey!!! Me again at eighteen months old. My new teeth are coming in.

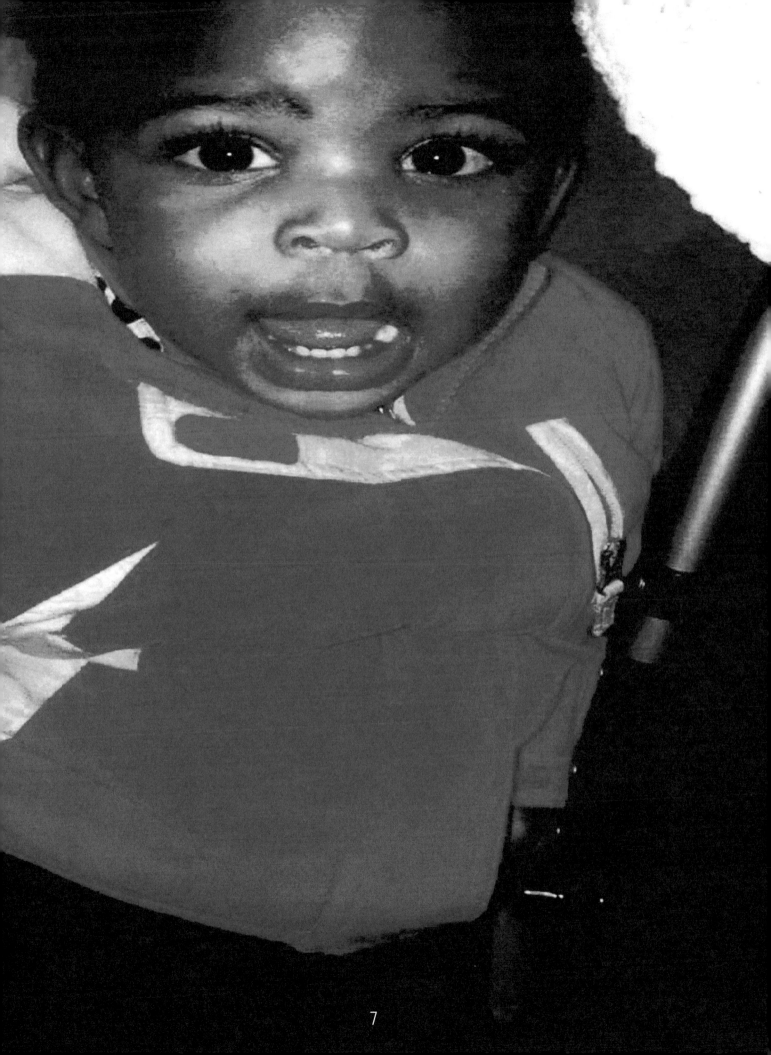

My Aunt Trina is always talking about ways to make money. I am sharing this story to teach other children my age how I save my first $5,050. Aunt Trina put the money on a table to count it. It was $56.00.

The next day

"Nova! I want to teach you how to save money by the time you are eighteen years old. Are you feeling better today?" Aunt Trina said. I responded yes. We went to the fruit market and picked out some pineapples, with the $56.

We looked at different apples. I also learned apples have different prices. They are red ones. Green ones. Some were $3.99. Some were $4.99.

We saw watermelons red ones and yellow ones. I even pick up a pumpkin.

We had a party for my sister and my cousin at his house.

After the fruit market

We went to the bank. Aunt Trina put the money on the counter for me to learn how to count. It was $300. I placed it in my secret envelope and put it away. This was the day I started to save money.

Later that night

Aunt Trina said "WHATEVER YOU DO DON'T TOUCH THIS ENVELOPE UNTIL THE END. IF YOU DON'T TOUCH IT, IT SHOULD ADD UP TO FIVE THOUSAND FIFTY DOLLARS FOR SIX MONTHS." I actually started thinking about what she was saying to me.

21

Printed in the United States
by Baker & Taylor Publisher Services